Wicked Wigan 2

Stories of horror, cruelty, crime and suffering in EDWARDIAN WIGAN

by
Geoffrey Shryhane

MALBON BOOKS

First published October 1994

Malbon Books
Gathurst
Wigan

The copyright to the contents of this book is held by Geoffrey Shryhane and may not be reproduced in any form without the permission of the author

A CIP catalogue record for this book is available from the British Library.
ISBN: 0 9517717 4 4

Printed by: The Hallgate Press,
Eckersley's No 3 Mill
Swan Meadow Road
Wigan

Wicked Wigan 2 ...

This is my fifth book. By a Wiganer, about Wigan and for Wiganers.

Wicked Wigan was last year's Christmas best seller. In fact, it sold out two weeks before Santa arrived. It dealt with murder, cruelty, crime and suffering in Wigan in Victorian times.

Wicked Wigan was re-printed in February.

The success of the book - and I hold the view that readers are far more important than writers - did not take long to persuade me that there was room to continue this theme.

So I have and have taken the stories from the Edwardian days.

Without doubt, the suffering was continuing, despite giant strides in communication and improved public health and social facilities.

There is evidence that Queen Victoria passed through Wigan many times on her way to Scotland, by train. She was so impressed, if that is the right word, by the evidence of industrious hard work that she commissioned a famous artist of the time to portray the belching smoke-stacks of the time on canvas.

The artist L S Lowry was a teenager in the Edwardian years. He would paint the scene a decade later. But like the Queen, passing through at speed, his portrayals of the mills and the matchstick men, while vibrant, were unconcerned with the real poverty and the real sufferings of the people.

Wicked Wigan - Vol 2 - peeps into those Edwardian years and into the lives of those whose realities are now but a memory in fading files and dusty old reports.

Geoffrey Shryhane

GEOFFREY SHRYHANE: Now Assistant Editor of the Wigan Observer and Wigan Reporter, Geoff has spent his 34 years as a newspaper reporter in his home town. After being Chief Reporter of the Observer for almost 20 years, his promotion came in October last year when the two local newspapers amalgamated. In 1992, he was given a "Feature Writer of the Year" award for his series of articles on a Wigan born opera singer who spied for her country during the war.

Last year, his report on the problems and delights of amalgamating newspapers received the "Team of the Year" award from Lancashire Publications. Before Christmas he was given a "Services to the Community Award" by Hindley Rotary Club for his contribution to Wigan journalism.

Now concentrating on leader and feature writing, Geoff is planning a book to mark his 35 years as a local newspaper reporter.

Dedicated to my nephews and niece

**Victoria Wolstenholme
James Chapman
Christopher Wolstenholme**

* The "Malbon" in **MALBON BOOKS** is the kennel name of our pet whippet "Pooky" (named after Jim Davis's cartoon cat, Garfield). Pooky, a blue whippet, has the kennel name "Malbon Lazuli." She is seven.

Acknowledgements

Mark Ashley, Observer and Reporter MD - "OK. Do another."

My wife Peggy - "Are you typing up there all night?"

Bob McWilliam, who helped carry crumbling mite-infested files.

David Mottler (Hallgate Press) - "Get the manuscript in on time."

Kath Walker, illustrator - "Wigan really was VERY wicked."

My thanks to everyone concerned in producing the front cover photo.

Vic Jolley Photography, Fleet Street Pemberton for the use of his studio and photographic expertise.

Pierhead Gates & Welding Co. Eckersley No. 3 Mill, Swan Meadow Road, for the ornamental gates.

Brian, John and Sid for posing in the photo.

'Standards,' The Wiend, Wigan, for the loan of the masks.

By the same author:
Wigan & Wiganers (1990)
Peering at Wigan (1991)
Window on Wigan (1992)
Wicked Wigan (1993)

**Main Illustrations
by Kath Walker**

EDWARDIAN TRAGEDIES

ROBBERIES FROM PEMBERTON FARMS.
BANK HOLIDAY OFFENCES.

At the Wigan Borough Police Court, on Monday, before Messrs. S. Melling, T. Fyans, W. Rigby, and J. Hilton, Anthony Solon, of no settled address, was charged with breaking and entering Highfield House Farm and stealing a gold albert, a five dollar gold piece, half a dozen dessert knives, half a dozen dessert forks, half a dozen dinner forks, two pairs of kid gloves, a silver brooch, and four studs, value £8 10s., the property of James Ackers, on the 6th August.

The Chief Constable said some of the articles were in pledge at Liverpool, and they wished to recover as much of the property as possible. Prisoner was found in a public house in Worsley Mesnes trying to dispose of some knives. He would offer sufficient evidence to justify a remand. There was also another case. He used to work on a farm at Winstanley, and whilst Winstanley Flower Show was on last Monday prisoner, knowing that the farmers and their families went to the show, he took advantage of their absence and broke into two farm houses.

Police-constable Moore said at ten minutes past seven on Saturday night, from something said to him, he went to the Tippings's Arms and found Solon there with a lot of knives and forks on the table. He was trying to sell them, and witness had since found they were the proceeds of a robbery from Highfield Farm. When arrested and charged, he said, "Some of them."

He was remanded until Monday.

THE WIGAN WIFE WOUNDING CASE.
DRIVEN TO DESPERATION.

On Tuesday, at the Liverpool Assizes, Robert Halsall, 52, carter, was brought before Mr. Justice Lawrence in the Crown Court for sentence, he having last week been found guilty of wounding his wife, Mary Ann Halsall, with intent to do her grievous bodily harm at Wigan on the 9th June.

His Lordship said he had some considerable difficulty in knowing how to deal with the prisoner's case. The learned counsel who so ably defended him did what he could on his behalf. There were circumstances in the

THE MORTALITY RETURNS.

The Registrar-General reports that the deaths in 76 large towns in England and Wales last week averaged 18·4 per thousand per annum. In the preceding three weeks the rates had been 13·8, 14·6, and 17·0. The rates for the following towns are:—

Barrow-in-Furness	11·1	Newcastle-on-Tyne	15·1
Birkenhead	24·9	Nottingham	23·4
Birmingham	22·9	Northampton	11·1
Blackburn	13·6	Oldham	20·0
Bolton	16·2	Preston	13·9
Bradford	17·0	Rochdale	16·1
Bristol	13·2	Rotherham	18·5
Burnley	15·2	Salford	20·0
Bury	12·4	Sheffield	21·1
Cardiff	12·8	South Shields	19·7
Derby	14·7	Stockport	28·3
Gateshead	14·4	St. Helens	20·0
Grimsby	20·3	Stockton-on-Tees	19·8
Halifax	11·9	Sunderland	18·2
Huddersfield	16·5	Tynemouth	19·3
Hull	21·7	Warrington	15·1
Leeds	19·0	West Hartlepool	13·5
Leicester	18·9	Wigan	29·2
Liverpool	24·2	Wolverhampton	16·9
Manchester	22·3	York	12·5
Middlesbrough	20·3		

The rate in London was 18·3, Edinburgh 12·2, Glasgow 14·4, Dublin 21·5, and Belfast 19·8.

PECULIAR DEATH OF A WIGAN DATALLER.

The death of Richard Myers, a dataller, 59 years of age, is reported under peculiar circumstances. It appears that the deceased was resident with his daughter, Esther Myers, at 65, Bottling Wood, and left home on Monday morning to go to his work at the Douglas Bank Collieries in his usual state of health. At half-past four in the afternoon he came to the pit eye, and along with others got into the cage and was wound to the surface. Prior to arriving at the top, however, two men noticed deceased hanging over a bar at the side of the cage, and pulled him in. On reaching the pit bank it was found that the man was unconscious, and Dr. McElligott was sent for. The doctor, on his arrival, found the man dying. He was removed home in the ambulance.

HINDLEY WIFE KILLING CASE

Peter Turner, 24 years of age, a collier, who lived at Bolton's Yard, Hindley, appeared at Liverpool Crown Court charged with having murdered his wife Martha on 20th May (1904) by striking her on the head with a poker. It was a case which had attracted a vast amount of interest in Hindley where the parties were well-known and there was a fair number of people from that neighbourhood present in court who followed the proceedings with the keenest interest.

The prosecution was in the hands of Mr Maxwell and the defendant was represented by Mr Shawcross.

Turner was brought up to the dock and pleaded not guilty. He had a haggard look and also appeared somewhat changed owing to his hair having considerably grown during the time of waiting for the trial.

His white and nervous hands told their own story of a life away from pit work. Generally he sat on the chair in a very despondent attitude looking in a most miserable frame of mind. When any special reference was made to his wife he sobbed bitterly.

Mr Maxwell opened the case by acquainting the jury with the facts. He said that the prisoner and his wife were living in Bolton's Yard, but it was not known on what terms. The deceased was perfectly well that night and had been to see her mother.

At half past ten on the night in question, a witness named Atherton saw the prisoner and he was the worse for drink. They did not know what took place when they were in the house together that night but Atherton heard screams and the prisoner's wife said her husband had thrown a paraffin lamp at her.

When the woman was seen lying unconscious, he said "I don't know what I've done it for." He agreed his wife was "a good wench."

On the following morning, prisoner went to his wife's parents' house and told them what he had done and that he had struck her with the poker.

John Atherton, collier, of Granby Street, said his house backed on to Bolton's Yard and on the night in question said the prisoner was in drink. He was staggering, but not staggering all over the road. He went into his home. Minutes later, Mrs Turner arrived screaming. She said the prisoner had thrown a lamp at her. She had called him a monkey. He had taken a running kick at her. He wore clogs.

Shortly afterwards, witness went on an errand and saw Mrs Turner at the top of the entry looking frightened. She said she could not get into her own home, so he took her to his. A bit later, the prisoner arrived, thumping at the door and breaking the windows. Witness took the prisoner home and told him if he would be quiet, he would fetch his wife to him. He agreed. Prisoner's wife went home and a minute after he followed, but a yard or two from the door he heard deceased scream "Oh Pe. Don't. Don't lad. Don't." Witness got into the house and found the woman lying on her back on the floor, a bleeding wound on her head. A poker lay nearby. She was unconscious. He asked the prisoner why he had done it and he said he did not know. He agreed that his wife was a quiet woman.

Mrs Atherton arrived and she and the witness put the woman on the sofa and dressed the wound as well as they could. It was about three o'clock when they left. All this time, the prisoner was sitting on a chair by the fire. He was

crying and did not help. There was much blood in the house.

Mr Shawcross said the prisoner, an industrious man, worked at the Eatock Pit of the Wigan Coal and Iron Company.

Mary Ann Marsh, mother of the deceased, gave her evidence crying. She was accommodated with a seat in the witness box. She said her daughter had supper with her on the night of the 28th and the next morning the prisoner arrived. She asked where Martha was. He started crying and witness asked if he had been beating her again and he said "Yes, I have done more than ever I have done in my life. I have hit her on the head with the poker. She had never spoke since."

Alice Dootson of Lower Leigh Road, Daisy Hill, Westhoughton, said she used to live next door to the Turners. They were there last Christmas. Witness said she saw the prisoner beat his wife once. She saw him push and kick her. When witness asked why he had done it, he said it was because she was always out of the house. On that occasion the woman ran into the house and the prisoner followed her. There was a scream and she cried out "Oh mother" and he shouted "I'll make it so tha can't shout 'Oh mother.'"

Dr Bowan of Hindley gave evidence that there was a wound over the left ear communicating directly with the brain. In his opinion a poker could have caused the death wound.

By Mr Shawcross: In his opinion, a fall against a nail in the door would not cause the wound. Nor would the latch.

Mr Maxwell summed up for the prosecution and then Mr Shawcross for the defence, saying it was a sad case because Turner was a young man on the threshold of life. He was a good worker. The question the jury had to decide was if the prisoner inflicted the wounds to the head.

The jury retired and after 50 minutes, returned and the prisoner was again brought to the dock. He stood, pale, nervous and distressed, his gaze directed on the foreman of the jury.

The jury was counted by the clerk amid almost painful silence and then the foreman asked at what verdict they had arrived.

"Manslaughter" was the reply.

The prisoner stood with a relieved expression on his features. The judge told him he had been found guilty under circumstances which made it clear that the jury had taken a very lenient view of his conduct. He accepted the view the jury had taken that he had committed the crime under the influence of drink but the crime was so serious, he felt bound to pass upon him a sentence of ten years penal servitude.

Prisoner had stood quiet and erect all this time and as soon as he heard the sentence, up went his hands to give a salute of thanks and those near enough heard him say "Thanks, your worship." He turned round with a springy tread and left the dock and went down the steps to the cells below with an air of greatest satisfaction.

This was the conclusion of the case and the parties interested streamed out of court.

SEVEN LIVING IN CELLAR

A shocking example of the conditions under which some people live was shown during the hearing of a case at the Wigan Borough Police Court on Thursday. John Moran, of 18 Great George Street and his wife, were summoned for neglecting their five children between 1st January and 18th March (1904).

Mrs Moran did not appear.

Mr Lees, who prosecuted on behalf of the National Society for the Prevention of Cruelty to Children, stated that the woman was in the workhouse. It was a very sad case indeed. Defendant was a joiner but owing to his lazy, drunken habits, he would not work regularly and for five months the wife and children had been reduced to the utmost poverty. They had very little clothing and on the 5th inst. they were ejected from their house in Clayton Street, Wigan, and since then and up to the visit of the Union Officer, they had been in a cellar in Great George Street, Wigan. The place was 8ft. by 8ft. and about 8ft high and the only furniture was an old sofa and two wooden stools. Defendant, his wife and five children, the eldest being 15, all slept together on a mattress on the floor. They had been asked to go into the workhouse from time to time but they had refused. Since the summons had been issued, the woman and children had gone into the institution. The Society thought it was a case that the man should go into the workhouse until the children had recovered their health, as at present they were in a shocking state.

The Court heard that the defendant was able-bodied and they did not want able-bodied men in the workhouse.

The Justices agreed that the wife and children remain in the workhouse and that Moran be sent to prison for three months.

MARGARINE FOR BUTTER

Oliver Egan (or McKinley), grocer, of 49 Darlington Street, Wigan, was charged on three counts at Bradford Police Court with selling margarine at a shop known as "McKinley's Irish Butter Market" in Westgate, Bradford. Only one charge went ahead and to this he pleaded guilty.

Mr W G Purnell, who prosecuted, said he believed the prisoner had been concerned in carrying out an extensive fraud all over the north of England.

A man named Kelly, who was in the shop in Bradford, had already been dealt with by the Court for a similar offence and when the Food Inspector visited the shop, the prisoner had cleared off.

The police, said Mr Purnell, had difficulty in tracing him but he was found in the shop at Wigan. But another wanted man had managed to escape.

Mr Newell, who defended, said his client had been duped by another man.

The Stipendiary, who said he had no doubt that this was one of a series of long term frauds through the country, inflicted a fine of £25 and £1 costs on the accused, with an alternative of a month in prison.

ELDERLY IN COURT
PRISONER AT 75

William Fairhurst, of 8 Schofield Lane, Wigan, certainly had the appearance of having weathered storms of many years when he appeared before the Wigan Court.

He was in the dock charged with unlawfully wounding his wife, aged 70.

The Chief Constable said that the previous night, the couple had a glass of beer together and went to bed. They had words and he took up an iron bolt and struck her in the face, causing injuries she was now suffering from.

The woman was desirous of not pressing the case. It seemed a pity that two persons of their age should be in such a position.

The complainant, whose husband's head was bandaged when he appeared in court, said he was only strange when he had a drop to drink.

Alderman Richards, who was one of the Magistrates, said he had known the couple for the whole of his life and was extremely sorry to see them there.

The Chief Constable, answering the Chairman, said the man had a number of convictions for selling "slink" (prematurely born) meat.

Complainant "That is o'er and past. (Laughter).

Asked by the Chairman, Mr O Rushton what he had to say in his defence, the prisoner replied "I getten drunk." (Laughter).

Complainant asked to be allowed to withdraw the charge and this the Court allowed but told the defendant to conduct himself better in the future.

WIGAN COUNTY POLICE COURT (1902)

GIRL COAL PICKER: A 14 year old girl named Edith Cox of Abram was summoned for stealing a quantity of coal worth five pence (2p) from the Abram Colliery Company on 11th August 1902. Mr Allen (Messrs Peace and Ellis) represented the company and said they had a great deal of trouble with people picking coal at the colliery siding. The girl had gone there for no other reason than to steal coal which had been jolted from the wagons and the company desired to put a stop to that sort of thing. Asked by an officer why she was stealing, she said her father was out of work and she was very sorry. They were very cold. The case was adjourned so the father could be summoned.

DAMAGE TO A FARM: Wm Heaton and John Unsworth of Pemberton admitted damaging a field of vetches (plant of the pea family) the property of W L White to the amount of one shilling (5p). Complainant said the defendants had trampled in the field and so damaged the vetches. Defendants were ordered to pay the damage and five shillings (25p) costs.

FROM PILLAR TO POST: Richard Pickering, 23, of Ashton, was summoned by his wife for persistent cruelty to her, causing her to leave him. Eliza Pickering, 20, said she left her husband on Friday because of his cruelty to her the previous night when he thumped her on the head and also because he told her she had to go. He had assaulted her many times before. In answer to Mr T Wilson, who appeared for the defendant, she said they had only been married for 15 months and admitted that on the previous Thursday she hit him with a jug because he had thumped her. She also complained that he had never found her a home since they married but had had her in lodgings from pillar to post. The case was adjourned for a month to see if the parties could come to some agreement.

HE WAS NOT ALWAYS DRUNK: Eliza Bethell of Hindley accused her husband Richard, to whom she had been married for 15 years, with persistent cruelty to her and said he was not always drunk but got intoxicated as often as he could. He was "agate" of her on Friday and Saturday night. It was six weeks since they had a good fight - they had a fight every time he had any money. The case was dismissed.

NUISANCE CAUSED BY FOWL: Levi Catterall of 120 Hardybutts, Wigan, was charged with committing a nuisance on his premises by keeping poultry and pigeons. Mrs Catterall told the Justices that it was true they kept them, but had now got without them. Mr Sumner, the sanitary inspector, said that in July he visited the house and found it in a disgraceful condition due to the keeping of pigeons and poultry. He served a notice but when visiting a week later, found the scandalous state still existed. A summons was taken out. The Magistrates made an order for the nuisance to be removed within three days and fined the defendant two shillings (10p)

CHILDREN EATING HORSE BEANS: Some pitiful details were brought out in a case at Wigan Court. Ralph Headley of Aspull was charged with neglecting his four children. Mr Hall prosecuted for the NSPCC. Prisoner, he alleged, had been living in and out of different workhouses for some time: he would not work and his family had to go out begging whilst he was drinking and lounging about. He was absolutely incorrigible and lazy. Police Constable Innies spoke of warning the prisoner on several occasions. When he visited the house he found the surroundings squalid and filthy and the children, who were without food, had for the previous three months been dependent on the charity of neighbours. They had started to steal out of sheer hunger. A man called Westby gave evidence as to the prisoner's laziness and a witness named Jones spoke of finding Headley's two sons in a stable, so hungry they were eating horse beans. Inspector Ford (NSPCC) said on one occasion when he called, he was told the family had lived on bread and salt for a week. The children were dressed in rags. Prisoner was sent to gaol for three months with hard labour.

REFUSING TO QUIT: Robert Gibson, 72, of Hallgate, pleaded guilty to a charge of being drunk and refusing to quit the Globe Inn when requested to do so on Saturday night. Detective Inspector Fearn said he visited the public house and saw the defendant drunk in the lobby. The landlord ordered him out but five minutes later found he had gone back. They took him into custody. A fine of ten shillings (50p) was imposed.

DISGRACE OF STREET FOOTBALL: For playing football in Schofield Lane, Wigan, John Ratcliffe was ordered to pay costs. The Magistrate said the court was determined to stamp out such nuisances.

CHARGE AND COUNTER CHARGE: Mary Lythgoe, of Ashton, was summoned for using profane language to Eliza Pickering but the case was dismissed. Mrs Pickering was also accused by the previous defendant with assaulting her, the complainant saying she received a rap on the face in her own house "which, on my heart is true , even if I might die in a minute."

The Magistrates dismissed that case also.

SLEEPING IN WAITING ROOM: An elderly man called William Cawley of no settled address, who was formerly a porter, was found and charged with sleeping in the waiting room at Wigan Station without having any visible means of subsistence. At 11-30 on Saturday night, the man was noticed to go through the luggage subway on the station and as he did not come back a search was made. He was found sleeping in the waiting room on No 5 Platform with his jacket rolled up as a pillow. He was sent to prison for seven days.

The court rose in the mid afternoon.

STRANGE DEATH OF FARM LABOURER

Thomas Walsh, 61, a farm labourer, died under peculiar circumstances on Monday. He worked for Moses Phythian, of the Glass House Farm, Park Lane, Pemberton, and had been allowed to sleep in one of the barns. On the previous Monday he was found unconscious on the ground near the barn with a wound at the back of the head. He tried but could not restore him although he visited him several times.

An inquest was held at the Ben Johnson Inn, Goose Green, the following day. The first witness was the brother Dennis, of 47 Brackley Street, Goose Green, who said the deceased had no settled residence but used to work on farms and sleep in barns. This he had done for several years.

Moses Phythian said Walsh had worked for him for a year and slept in the loft over the shippen which he reached from the yard by way of ladder.

On Monday morning at about 6-30 he found him lying as described.

Coroner: What worries me is that you did not call anybody in until quarter to eleven.

Witness: I called in another workman.

Coroner: But didn't you see how bad he was?
Witness: No. When I found him he was snoring.
Coroner: Was there any blood about?
Witness: I did not see any.
Coroner: Was anybody present when he died?
Witness: No.
Continuing witness said he thought the deceased had tried to get into the loft without using the ladder and had fallen.

Police Constable Powell said on searching the deceased's clothes, he found a shilling (5p) and there was a wound one and a half inches long at the back of his head. The skull was fractured.

The foreman of the jury expressed the opinion that when men slept in lofts, there should be some provision made for their entrance and exit.

The Coroner said he had once discussed with a farmer the matter of allowing labourers to sleep in lofts. The farmer said there was a good deal of sense in it. That if they did not sleep in the barns there was no way of knowing what damage the men may do to his crops or what damage they would do with a match for instance.

Verdict: Accidental death.

DANGERS OF THE DOLLY TUB

Another has been added to the already long list of juvenile victims to the wash tub. Another child has been drowned in the dolly tub in this district - this time at Hindley. Its name was Charles Simm and it was the year and ten months old son of Samuel Simm of 5 Martin Street, Hindley. An inquest was held by Coroner Mr Brighouse at the Royal Hotel, Hindley, on Tuesday (1902). The mother, Ellen Simm, described how the infant met with its death. It was playing in the yard, she said, trying to sail a salmon tin in some water that was in a tub. When it had been out of the house about a quarter of an hour, she looked and discovered it head downwards in the tub. The infant had fallen into the water while endeavouring to reach the can, which was also in the water. Artificial respiration was tried, but without avail. The tub was nineteen inches long and fourteen inches wide and at the time it contained only six inches of water. A verdict of Accidental Death was returned.

THE MISSING HINDLEY WOMAN.

The above is the portrait of the young married woman, Edith Alice Taylor, of Castle Hill, who is reported missing. She left her home about half-past nine on the morning of November 18th last, and from that day to this nothing has been seen or heard of her. The police have made exhaustive enquiries to trace her but with no success, and notices have been posted up and down the district, and also in other towns, but with a similar result. The description given is that she is 27 years of age, 5ft. 5½in. in height, dark brown hair, and blue eyes. She was wearing a blue mingled skirt, black bodice, blue shawl over shoulders, black shawl over her head and buttoned boots. There is nothing to account for her disappearance, and a reward is offered to any person giving information which will lead to her discovery.

PET NAMES

A woman named Cissie McDonald, of 38 Bolton Street, was summoned at the Wigan Borough Police Court on Monday (1904) for assaulting Elizabeth A Parker, her next door neighbour.

Complainant said that on Wednesday morning, Mrs McDonald gave her a "tup" and dragged her by the hair across the floor and bruised her elbow. Her children were always spreading sand about the entry and she had complained. That was the fourth time she had beaten her.

Defendant: Every time I go out, don't you call me "gravy eyes?." (Laughter).

Complainant: Yes, but she calls me "cockroach face." (Laughter).

A daughter of the defendant said the complainant went into the house and she and her mother got to fighting with their fists on the floor and also kicking and scratching each other. This happened a lot.

The Bench ordered the parties to divide their own costs.

SWALLOWING LEAD MONKEY
LUCKY BAG LEADS TO DEATH

Mr Milligan, the Coroner, held an inquest at Wigan Infirmary on Lily Smith, aged three, who died there the previous day after swallowing a lead monkey which stuck in her throat five days before.

Albert Smith, collier, said his daughter bought a halfpenny lucky bag containing a lead monkey among the sweets. He said the lead monkey was stuck in the child's mouth and her mother tried to get it out, but couldn't so they sent for Dr Pollard who ordered her to the Infirmary. The girl could not swallow anything. Every time she tried, she started screaming. The child had bought lucky bags before. All the children did. It was understood that the lead toy was got out at the hospital.

Coroner: It is a pity that the child was not brought to the Infirmary at once.

Witness: We put off bringing her in the expectation that the child would get rid of it, as the doctor thought she might.

Miss Derbyshire, a shopkeeper, said she bought the bags from a traveller. Some people called them hidden treasure packets.

Coroner: Well, the treasure is easier found in these than in some other places where the treasure has been hidden. (Laughter).

Coroner, to Miss Derbyshire: We cannot blame you for selling them.

He added that no one person was to blame.

COLLIER'S JEALOUSY

At the Liverpool Assizes on Wednesday (1904), a collier named Thomas Meakin, aged 38, of Ince-in-Makerfield pleaded guilty to shooting with a pistol at another collier named Patrick Frane with murderous intent.

The Judge heard that the prisoner was very sorry. His Lordship trusted that the prisoner fully realised what he had nearly done. Had he killed him, he would have ended his life on the gallows. Prisoner seemed to have fancied that he had provocation and he (the judge) said he had some sympathy with a man who showed his fondness for his wife. But in Meakin's case drink had also something to with the crime.

He was sent to prison for four months.

THRASH THESE BOYS

Last Friday (1905) two boys evidently with the idea of providing their own sensationalism, told a remarkable story to Wigan Police. They said they saw a well-dressed man throw a child he'd been carrying into a stream in Wallgate which at that time was swollen with the heavy rain. It was a tributary of the River Douglas. So graphic were their descriptions and so minutely did they detail what had taken place that the police authorities considered that there was something in their story.

The boys even went so far as to say that the child cried "Oh Father, don't" but the man replied "You must go" and then pitched him into the water.

A sergeant and two officers then went to the place and started dragging operations. Nothing resulted. Being suspicious, one of the officers took the lads to the place a little later and after impressing on them the seriousness of the situation, the two sensationalists admitted they had been telling falsehoods and that the whole story was a fabrication.

Without doubt it was a most singular thing for lads of 10 or 11 years of age to do, but perhaps the perusal of sensational literature may account for it in some way.

We don't suppose they have committed any offence against the law but a good thrashing would certainly not be out of place.

COMPENSATION FOR INSANITY

At the Wigan County Court on Tuesday (August 1902) before his honour Judge Bradbury, Abraham Hilton, a collier of 204 Scot Lane, Pemberton, claimed 20 shillings (£1) a week for compensation from the Rosebridge and Douglas Bank Colliery Company, on behalf of his son, Joseph, at present of unsound mind.

From the statement of claim, it appeared that the son, while working as a collier in South Pit, Wigan, on 15th January, last was struck on the head by a large piece of falling coal with the result that serious injury was sustained, causing him to become of unsound mind shortly afterwards.

Mr T Wilson, represented the applicant, and Mr A Ellis appeared for the company.

Mr Wilson said the applicant was a single man and when working was the chief support of his family. The amount of compensation agreed upon was 15 shillings and four pence a week (72p) and he applied now that His Honour should give compensation of that amount.

The son was an inmate of Rainhill Asylum and, of course, the father was responsible for his keep while there.

Mr Wilson said it was a case of total incapacity and they wanted half the man's earnings

This the judge agreed to the settlement.

UP HOLLAND HAUNTED HOUSE

The usual quiet district at Up Holland has been all agog with excitement for some days and nights in consequence of some unseen noises and odd happenings in the centre of the village. In fact, it is so mysterious that the house in which they have manifested themselves, has attained the reputation of being haunted. The house which is occupied by a widow, Mrs Winstanley, and her family of four sons and three daughters overlooks the churchyard and is almost opposite the grave of George Lyon, the notorious Up Holland highway man who was hanged at the start of the last century at Lancaster and afterwards, his body brought home for burial.

The haunted house is next door to the White Lion and is a centuries old stone structure. The walls are feet thick. All the day, through the doings of the mysterious agency are the talk of the township and as nightfall comes round, the approaches to the house are thronged with people who wait patiently for the supposed spiritual manifestations. The noises were first heard on Sunday night (August 1904) in one of the upstairs bedrooms. Knocking and rumblings in the wall were heard and these seemed to travel in the direction of a window which was walled up to avoid window tax many years previously. The window recess is now used as a sort of cupboard and two large books rest within.

When the noises were first heard, the occupants of the bed, three youths, so it is said, were awakened. A fear seized upon them and this was not all abated when the hanging was taken from the wall space and placed over their heads like a pall and the paper was torn from the wall and patches of hard mortar scattered about the room. Then the stones under the window board at the bottom of the cupboard were loosened and flung on to the floor. Matters seemed to be getting serious now and the rumours of the happenings in the house got about. Large crowds began to gather each night. It is only in the darkness and in the presence of one of the lads that the ghost operates.

THE " HAUNTED " CHAMBER.

THE " HAUNTED " HOUSE AT UPHOLLAND.

A local councillor in the person of Mr Baxter has been in the room on most of the occasions when the noises were heard and he is greatly puzzled as to the cause. He has searched inside and out and has had a brick-setter to examine the walls. When the stones fall, they are put back and wedged tightly so they could not be pulled out by hand, as soon as the light is turned down, the noises start again and the stones tumble to the floor.

Indeed so great is the thumping of the stones on the board floor that people 60 yards away can hear the noise.

So far all is a mystery. The crowd gathering increases every night as dusk comes on and people sit on the churchyard wall waiting for the "ghost" to start its nightly performance.

* At Wigan County Police Court Moses Gaskell and Henry Heyes were charged with being drunk and disorderly at Up Holland. The justices heard that the men were creating a disturbance near the haunted house. At least 2,000 people had gathered. But the defendants would not be quietened down. The men were fined one shilling (5p)

EDWARDIAN RIOTS

A CHAT ABOUT TEETH.

Desiring to centralise their already extensive business in Wigan and district, Messrs. Brown Bros. beg to intimate that they have taken the premises lately occupied by Messrs. Green and Langford, Standishgate, Wigan. The premises have been thoroughly modernised, and are now well adapted for the business. There is every convenience, and they confidently hope to retain all their old clients, and by strict and personal attention to greatly enlarge on their connection. The extraction of teeth has been made a study, and they now absolutely guarantee that all teeth will be extracted without pain. A trial is solicited, and they need hardly say that they guarantee satisfaction. Remember the address, Messrs. Brown Bros., 12, Standishgate, Wigan.

PET NAMES.

TERMS OF ENDEARMENT IN BOLTON STREET.

A woman named Cissie McDonald, of 38, Bolton-street, was summoned at the Wigan Borough Police Court on Monday for assaulting Elizabeth A. Parker, of 40, Bolton street, on the 5th inst.

Complainant said on Wednesday morning Mrs. McDonald gave her a tup and dragged her by the hair across the floor, and bruised her elbow. Her children were always spreading sand about the entry and she had complained. That was the fourth time she had beaten her.

Defendant: Every time I go out don't you call me "gravy eyes." (Laughter.)

Complainant: Yes, but she calls me "cockroach face." (Laughter.)

A daughter of the defendant said that complainant went into their house and she and her mother got fighting on the floor.

The bench ordered the parties to divide their own costs.

"WHITE GLOVES'" DAY AT THE WIGAN COUNTY POLICE COURT.

LESS CRIME IN THE COUNTY.

Again has a "White Gloves'" day occurred at the Wigan County Police Court. It was on Monday, and when the magistrates—Mr. Beazer, Mr. Sharrock, and Mr. Hartley—arrived on the bench they were informed by Superintendent Pincock that the list was free of cases.

Mr. Beazer said they were very glad to hear it.

Mr. James (assistant clerk): Following the usual custom, I have the pleasure of presenting you with a pair of white gloves as a mark of the absence of any crime. I believe this is the second pair you have had presented to you.

Mr. Beazer said that was so, and he was much obliged to Mr. James. He was very pleased that there was no work for the bench that day. During the last few years they had had a great deal less work in that court than formerly. He remembered the time when they used to sit until four or five o'clock on Friday afternoons, whereas they now very rarely attended after luncheon hour. But he thought they would agree with him that there was less crime in the county throughout, and especially in that district.

A CHORLEY SHOOTING CASE.

At the Liverpool Assizes on Saturday, Robert Fowler (46), labourer, was charged with having, on the 16th July, near Chorley, shot at John Kenny with a gun, with intent to do him grievous bodily harm.

Mr. M'Nab prosecuted, and Mr. Shee, Q.C., and Mr. Cavanagh appeared for the defence.

On the advice of Mr. Shee, the prisoner pleaded guilty to unlawfully wounding. Mr. Shee said he had studied the case carefully, and he had come to the conclusion that it was one in which they could not resist such a charge.

Mr. M'Nab thought the justice of the case would be met by such a verdict.

Mr. Shee said that prisoner was a hard-working man, and had been teased by a number of children. The gun was so loaded that he did not think he could do much harm with it. The prisoner's father, who was 73 years of age, had walked thirteen miles to attend the court and appear for his boy as he called him, and

DRUNKEN SCENES AT CARNEGIE LIBRARY

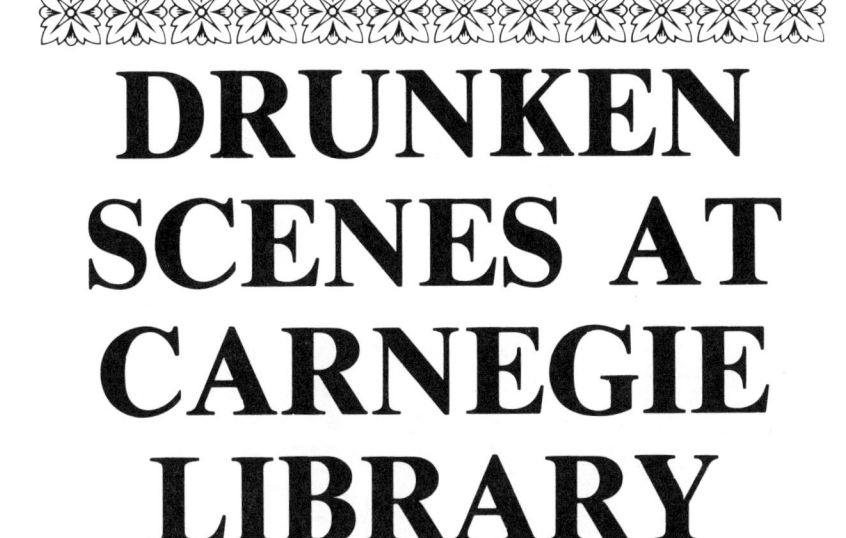

There were scenes of terrible fighting and drunkenness in the vicinity of the Carnegie Library late on Saturday night. The dreadful scene brought 35 policemen to the scene and people poured from their houses in order to watch the spectacle. Some people were even said to have left their beds to witness the carnage which involved over 100 men, many from other areas of Wigan.

An eye witness said that the district was quiet all evening, save for some people out to take the summer evening air. The trouble began to brew when the pubs closed and men old and young began to assemble outside the Carnegie Library. From reports circulating, it would appear that the atmosphere was happy and congenial until one particularly drunken man threw a brick which smashed a window of the library. Several men found the incident amusing, but others, proud of the building, are believed to have taken exception and it was then that the fighting broke out.

A great cry went up and police were on their way within a few minutes. At first a handful of officers attempted to quieten the men, but their numbers were too many and reinforcements were sent for. By this time, dozens of men were fighting and there was blood everywhere on the pavements. The sight was not a pretty one but it was obvious that many people watching were greatly entertained while others were disgusted and shouted for the men to be off and on their way. It was shocking that decent people should have to put up with such behaviour, especially when they had worked hard at their labours all week.

Well after midnight the police brought the fighting under control. By this time, the men who were the victims of drink but still able to function slunk away, some towards Wigan and others in the direction of Orrell. But others argued with the officers, defending their friends.

Police arrested about 20 of the men who are to appear in the Wigan Borough Police Court on charges of varying kinds.

A MINER'S NOISY WIFE

"I have had more rest this last fortnight than I have had for the last three of four weeks" were the words used by Robert Lee, of 73 Back Caroline Street, Ince, when charged at Wigan Borough Court on Thursday with deserting his wife, Margaret.

Mrs Lee said they had been married for 26 years and had six children, two of them being under 16 years of age. He left her over a fortnight ago and although she had seen him three times, he said he would not give her anything until he was made to.

Defendant: Did you not tell me on Sunday I would have to go?

His wife: No.

Defendant said she did. She preferred his two sons to him.

John Lee, a son, gave evidence.

In answer to his father, he said he did not hear his mother tell him to go.

Defendant alleged that one of his sons and a man gave him two punches one night. His wife was constantly drunk and he obtained no rest at nights.

Police Constable Burbridge said he knew complaintant as she had been before the court on several occasions for drunkenness and for smashing windows. Defendant was a quiet man who attended his work and had a lot of trouble with his two sons.

It was pointed out to the defendant that he would either have to contribute towards his wife's maintenance or go back.

He said he would go back and do his best.

Complainant, however, didn't desire this, so the magistrate thought they were better apart, and made an order for Lee to pay his wife 2s 6d (12p) a week and he should have custody of the two younger children.

TINNED SALMON LED TO DEATH

An inquest into the circumstances of the death of a youth named Albert Leonard, 18, a colliery drawer at Messrs Crompton and Shawcross's Pit, and residing in Bryn Street, Wigan, was held at the Borough Courts on Monday (1909) by Mr Milligan, the Borough Coroner.

The father, Frederick Leonard, said when the lad returned from work with him, he was apparently in good health. They had tea at about five o'clock. Deceased had the last bit of salmon, about as much as would cover a penny and then said he would rather have some boiled ham like the witness was having. Afterwards, he bought an ice cream sandwich and then went upstairs to change his clothes. He said he would stand his brother a half-penny worth of ice cream and they sent out for some more. Deceased only had a taste of his and said he could not eat it. He laid on the sofa and said he felt unwell. Witness asked him what was the matter and he said he felt a pain close to his heart. He persuaded him to have a walk and they went out together. When near Eckersley's Mill he leaned against the railings and began crying. He said he would go home and witness went on to get some brandy for him.

When he returned, he was dead.

Replying to the Coroner, witness said the others had salmon and were perfectly well after it. He had boiled ham and felt no ill effects and one of his younger daughters had the ice cream which deceased left. She was all right.

Elizabeth Dickinson, a neighbour said she had known deceased for 15 years and he was a strong lad. She saw him lying on the couch in some pain. He was crying. Some minutes later he died without the arrival of a doctor.

Dr Boyd said he made a postmortem examination and as he was told of the localised pain around the heart, began his examination in that region but found the heart normal. It would appear to him that there had been inflammation of the stomach. He knew the deceased had eaten fish before he died. He said that as his relatives had eaten the same, it could be a case of one man's "meat" was another man's poison.

The doctor said it was his view that the salmon was at the root of the matter. He suffered great pain and in his view, the cause of death was collapse, consequent upon acute pain from the inflammation.

The Coroner briefly summed up and the jury returned a verdict of death from natural causes.

FATALITY AT NEW THEATRE

Henry France, 46 years of age, a joiner employed by Mr D A Abbott, was engaged working on a scaffold at the New Theatre in King Street in Wigan when he fell to the ground. He was severely injured and was conveyed at once to the Wigan Infirmary where he died the following day.

Mr H Milligan, the Borough Coroner, held an inquest on the body at the Borough Courts and Mr J Gibson appeared on behalf of the widow, Mary France, of 135 Billinge Road, Pemberton, who gave evidence of identification, saying that her husband left home in the morning in his usual health. She was called to the Infirmary after the accident and saw her husband unconscious all the time. He never regained consciousness.

John Orrell, foreman for Mr Abbott, said the deceased was working in the circle of the new theatre. Witness was on the ground floor at about half past eight. The deceased fell almost at witnesses' feet, a distance of about 40 ft.

The deceased, who was a very active man, was perfectly sober at the time and the only thing he could account for the accident was that he stepped backwards while looking at some timber. The place was well lit by electric light. No-one actually saw him fall.

The Coroner said it appeared to be an accident and the jury returned a verdict of accidental death.

FALSE TEETH DEATH

At the Infirmary on Monday (July 1909) the Coroner held an inquest on a young woman named Elizabeth Macdonald who died early on Saturday morning. The circumstances were very unusual and brought up the question of whether patients should wear false teeth while in hospital.

The mother, Mary Macdonald, of Pool Street, Poolstock, said her daughter, who was unmarried, was rushed to the Infirmary suffering from appendicitis. When she went four days later she was told her daughter had died. She was just 21.

Mabel Stokes, a Wigan Infirmary nurse, said she was on duty and saw the deceased was getting better from her operation. Suddenly she heard a call and ran and found the deceased struggling as if in pain. She suddenly fell back, her mouth clenched. Witness pulled her mouth open and her tongue forward thinking Elizabeth was in a fit. Then she found her teeth were right in her throat. Witness got the teeth up but in a minute the girl died. She did not know she had false teeth.

Dr Batten, junior house surgeon, said the operation was a success but he was suddenly called by the night sister who said a very serious accident had happened. Artificial respiration was applied but it was no use. Asked about the cause of death, the doctor said he thought she died through the shock of her teeth going into her throat.

Coroner: What is the usual course to follow with patients with false teeth?

Doctor: For chloroform I always insist teeth are removed. I did in this case. She had a great desire to keep her teeth in. I do not know that the medical officer has a right, because there is no rule, to insist on the removal of false teeth.

Summing up, the Coroner said Elizabeth Macdonald was in a weak condition and would feel the shock more than an ordinary person and he thought people would agree that institutions should have the power to insist that the teeth of patients be removed. It would have saved this woman's life, at least for a few days.

DISORDERLY CONDUCT IN WORKHOUSE

PRISONER ROBBED DEAD BODY

A case which brings to mind the terrible railway accident at Wigan nearly 31 years ago was heard at Wigan Borough Police Court on Monday (1904) when an elderly man, named Ralph Rigby, who was then sentenced to ten years penal servitude for robbing a dead body at the station, was charged with being a disorderly pauper and damaging the property of the Workhouse Guardians. He pleaded not guilty.

Mr Alcock, the workhouse master, said the man was allowed out on Saturday but returned in the very early hours, very drunk and was put into the tramp cell. But he broke the bed and the window frame and got out.

The police had to be called and they locked him up. He appeared mad.

Prisoner alleged he was nearly choked and his head banged on the boards. Mr Alcock told him that he was beastly drunk.

A porter at the workhouse said the prisoner was more like a maniac. The Chief Constable said he had been attending court since he was 11 in 1855 when he made his first appearance. He had been whipped time after time and sent to a reformatory for five years but afterwards was continually going backwards and forwards to the assizes or sessions. He had twice served seven years and one term of ten years. In 1873 he had been convicted of stealing a gold watch from a body at a railway accident. The police always felt very pleased when he was at the workhouse because if he was out he was sure to be in mischief of some kind.

The Bench said discipline must be maintained in the Workhouse and he would have to go to prison for a month.

A PAIR OF WHITE GLOVES

There were no cases for hearing at the Wigan County Police Court on Monday morning and an old tradition was maintained when a pair of white gloves was presented to the presiding Magistrate, Mr Richard Johnson.

Superintendent O'Hara said he was very pleased to inform the Bench that there were no cases for hearing, especially as it was first meeting of the Court after the Coronation.

After the Coronation festivities, it augured well for the peace and goodwill of the people. It was not for want of energy on the part of the police that there were no cases for investigation but was attributable to the good conduct of the public.

Mr James, the Assistant Magistrates' Clerk, said he had great pleasure in presenting the white gloves. He congratulated his happy position that morning.

Mr Johnson said he was pleased to hear the words of Mr O'Hara had to say with regard to the good conduct of the people of the division and he thanked Mr James for the gloves, also congratulating all concerned.

He hoped it would be a good augury of a peaceful and happy reign for their King and Queen.

* The white gloves tradition has its roots in days when judges went out on circuit. It was customary to give judges white gloves which were provided by the High Sheriff. Items besides gloves were also presented.

When the Puritans had authority, they decreed that present giving cease but the judges and the High Sheriff, keen to maintain the pleasant old tradition, son the day.

What is odd is that the tradition of giving presents did not usually filter down to the lowly Magistrates' Courts. It can only be assumed that this happened in Wigan because some of the magistrates had ideas above their station.

SHOCKING ACCIDENT TO A CHILD

A sad fatality happened on Saturday afternoon (July 1906). The deceased was Bessie Havard who resided at Heart's Yard, Millgate. It appeared she was playing with some other children in Latham's Yard, Millgate, where there was a large plate glass case standing and which had been placed there by some workmen employed by Messrs Scott and Co., of Salford who were putting in a new shop window for the Maypole Dairy Company. The girl was trying to climb the case which had been placed against the wall and in doing so, she pulled it over on to herself. Two men near at the time lifted the case up and it was found that the child's skull had been fractured and life was extinct.

The Inquest

Mr Goffey, Deputy Borough Coroner, held the inquest at the Albion Hotel on Millgate. Mr Scott, owners of the case, was present.

Samuel Havard, father, gave evidence of identification and Sara Ann, sister, aged 10, said she was playing with other children around a box which was standing against the wall and some were climbing over it while others were behind pushing. There were a lot of them. A few of the children were running behind the box when there was only the deceased climbing on the front and it was caught behind and tilted over.

Coroner: How far was the box at the foot away from the wall?

Witness: Only an inch.

Coroner: Was there sufficient room for you to get behind it?

Witness: Yes, sideways

Continuing, witness said her sister was nearly at the top of the box when it fell.

John Bates, of 2 Latham's Yard said he was called from the house by a shout from one of the children. Earlier, he had seen them playing with the box and had asked them to go away but they took no notice of him. On hearing the child shout, he called Fred Kearsley and they both lifted the box up and found the deceased underneath it.

Edward Christian, foreman for Messrs Scott Bros, said he was in charge and had ascertained from Mr Hayes, electrician, that the yard was a private one and he had got permission to place the box there. He and others packed the box against the wall in such a manner as to make it impossible for it to be pulled over, even if two or three men were to climb on top. The packing underneath must have been removed.

Coroner: I think the explanation of the witness about the packing is perfectly satisfactory. Children must have kicked the packing away.

The jury returned a verdict of accidental death.

ARRESTED IN THE WORKHOUSE

A pitiful and sad case was heard before the Mayor, Alderman C B Holmes and other magistrates at the Wigan Borough Police Court.

A girl named Mary Ann Martindale, just 15 years of age, who had been a servant at a lodging house, was weeping in the dock charged with stealing a shawl.

The Chief Constable said the poor girl's behaviour was unstable owing to the way her mother and father had behaved. They were both in prison.

The girl had been employed as a domestic servant at a lodging house and while there, took the shawl worth one shilling and six pence (7p). She lost her position and in consequence was arrested in the Workhouse.

Certainly, the girl had no right to take the article but as she promised the court missionary that she would go into a home for two years, the case against her was withdrawn.

Mr Anders said the case was one of a wretched young girl whose life had been ruined because of the conduct of her parents.

TRAGIC DROWNING OF COLLIER

It was almost Christmas when William Connolly drank with a friend in a Wigan public house. But not long after, making his way home on a very dark night, he fell into the canal and drowned.

The body of Connolly, who lived at 180 Ince Green Lane, Ince, Wigan, was recovered from No 18 lock of the Leeds-Liverpool Canal about half past eight on Wednesday. He left home at five o'clock two days earlier and said he was going for a walk. It was the third week in December.

The deceased was seen in Wigan shortly afterwards and then nothing more was seen until his body was recovered.

The County Coroner, Mr Brighouse held an inquest at the Walmesley Arms, Higher Ince, and Mrs Connolly said her husband was 33 years of age.

James Gibson, a labourer, of 3 Lion Street, Wigan, said that at about seven o'clock on the Sunday night, he met Connolly in Scholes and they went to the Weaver's Arms and stayed about a quarter of an hour, having a pint of beer each. They then went to the Fleece Hotel and had three pints each.

Witness left at 8-30 and left Connolly in the hotel. He was perfectly sober and quite jovial. It was a very dark night.

Mr Abrams, the lock keeper told the inquest that at 8-30 in the morning, the body of Connolly was found in No 18 lock. It was towards the gates which could not be shut as a consequence that the body was found. It was very disfigured and the waistcoat and jacket were cut off.

The Coroner said it was a singular thing that the waistcoat and jacket were torn off but said he had conducted inquests where the man had no clothes on at all.

Police Sgt Waters said Connolly was a quiet man and had evidently got into the canal while going home.

The jury returned a verdict of found drowned.

PLATT BRIDGE CHILDS DEATH

An inquest was held at the Platt Bridge Inn, Platt Bridge, on Tuesday morning by Mr S Brighouse, the county coroner, on the body of an infant child named John Birchmore, son of Grace Birchmore, a single woman, of 40 Betley Street, Hindley.

The grandmother of the deceased said her daughter was 16 years of age last March. The deceased child was born on Thursday last and a certificated midwife had attended the mother. The deceased was taken to Dr Clark's surgery, but he was not in and a message was received at witness's house some time later that the child had died, the doctor not having seen it.

Dr Clark said he had examined the deceased and his opinion was that death was due from natural causes.

Police Inspector Ratcliffe stated that the mother of the deceased was of weak intellect.

A verdict was returned in accordance with the medical evidence.

TERRIBLE SAND PIT TRAGEDY

A terrible tragic happening took place on Wednesday morning in the sand pit when two young men, Lambert Highton, 18 years, of 11 Boyswell Lane and Robert Doran, 17, of 120 Whelley, suffocated by a terrible fall of sand while William Winnard, the son of the proprietor, had a miraculous escape.

It appears that the sand pits were worked by Winnards of Lorne Street and on the morning, his son and two young men were extracting sand to be carted away later on.

Suddenly, a very heavy fall of sand took place. Highton and Doran were completely buried but Winnard was only covered to the waist and was able to call for assistance.

Great difficulty was experienced in reaching the other two men as a tremendous heap of sand had to be removed and when discovered about an hour afterwards, their bodies were found lying together.

The calamity caused a great sensation in the district. It is a remarkable fact that this is the third fall of sand Winnard had been involved in.

The Inquest

Mr Milligan, the Coroner, held the inquest. Peter Doran said he was a collier and Robert was his son and a labourer employed by Mr Winnard. He had worked in the sand pit for about seven weeks. Harry Highton, a foundry labourer, said that his son had helped in the sand pit since leaving school.

The inquest heard that on the day in question, a slip of sand came at about 9-30 and the first fall caught them up to their knees. They were trying to be got out when a larger fall happened. Seven or eight tons fell. People came to the scene at once.

The Coroner asked William Winnard: How do you account for the sand slipping so often?

Witness said there must be slips in the sand strata.

Coroner: Do you use any prop?

Witness: You can't prop sand. If you did, it would slip out between the props.

Coroner: What have you done to prevent falls?

Witness: Sand slips many times when we are not there.

Coroner: So, shouldn't you take measures to prevent it?

Witness: Sand is dangerous wherever it is. There's nothing we can do.

Witness said he remembered a child being buried in the sand hold five years ago. Whatever you did, you could not keep them out.

The Coroner said the matters resolved themselves. It was a question of whether Mr Winnard had taken all reasonable precautions to prevent an accident. He obviously thought the place was safe. Now, the question was - had there been criminal negligence?

Accidental death verdicts were returned and the jury advised Mr Winnard to take every precaution in future to safeguard the lives of his men. The foreman added that in the opinion of the jury, the sand pit was left in a dangerous condition.

SCENE OF THE DISASTER.

CHRISTMAS DAY IN THE WORKHOUSE

It was Christmas Day in the Workhouse,
And the cold bare walls are bright
With garlands of green and holly,
And the place is a pleasant sight:
For with clean-washed hands and faces,
In a long and hungry line
The paupers sit at the tables
For this is the hour they dine.

**In the Workhouse: Christmas Day
By George R Sims (1847 - 1922)**

CHRISTMAS IN THE WIGAN WORKHOUSE (1906)

The inmates of the Union Workhouse in Wigan invariably find that Christmas day is made as happy as can be under the circumstances. The kindness of officials and friends makes the happiness perfect in many instances - in others it serves to mitigate the sorrow or brighten the gloom. Never were arrangements more complete at this institution for the passing of a contented if not a joyful day. The Guardians had given the usual permission for a special Christmas dinner and the master and matron, Mr and Mrs Alcock, with their usual care, saw to the comfort and convenience of the inmates. The day opened with divine service conducted by the Rector of Wigan.

Dinner was served at noon - regular, piping hot old-fashioned English fare, roast beef and vegetables and plum pudding and plenty of all. Those who wished beer had it. Those who preferred milk or mineral water were readily obliged. For this great feast, 618 lbs of beef were cooked.

Assembled to encourage the poor people to put them at their ease and participate in their gladness were the Mayor and Mayoress of Wigan.

The afternoon was given up to the customary enjoyments; fruit, tobacco and snuff being served. The children to the number of 50 were regaled with sweets and toys and in this instance there was no doubt as to the whole-heartedness of their enjoyment.

The day was brought to a close with a concert given by the officials assisted by certain of the inmates.

The master and matron desire to express their deep sense of obligation to those ladies and gentlemen of the town who have done so much for the poor living in the workhouse in Wigan.

CHRISTMASTIDE IN WIGAN (1906)

It was with surprise that most folks on awakening on Christmas morning found the weather, seasonable and of the old fashioned sort, the previous day had been muggy and gloomy with the ground beaten into a slush. And even reputed weather experts forecast a green Christmas. A sudden change upset all calculations and when Christmas morning dawned, there was a hoar frost on the window panes, the garden trees and the house tops. The ground too was frozen hard and there was ice on standing water.

The sudden change in the atmospheric conditions was a complete surprise to everybody and the seasonable weather was received with delight by the youngsters who used up their energy in making slides on the roadway. Christmas day was beautifully fine and clear, a cold nip in the air and the frozen ground thawing only where the sun was strongest.

Carol singers and choirs from the churches and chapels of the district paraded the streets after midnight on Christmas Eve had struck and during the night, the slumberer in dreams could hear the echo of festive music coming from outside. Special services were held.

Towards evening on Christmas Day, snow began to fall heavily and very soon the whole ground was carpeted with white to a depth of many inches.

So quickly did snow flakes fall that roadways were quickly blocked and traffic was greatly impeded. With the wind sweeping over the open country, drifts were soon formed in the deepest roads and on the way to Standish, the trams were early in trouble. From Boars Head to Standish village, the tramway lines were very early made impassable and cars on the route were snowbound and unable to continue their journey. In fact, the snowstorm disorganised the whole of the tram traffic and the services had to be suspended.

For many years, such a heavy fall of snow has not been experienced in Wigan. People on their way along the country lanes were in considerable difficulties and there are cases recorded where guests had to return and spend the night at the homes of their hosts through being snowed-up. Many passengers had to leave their snowbound cars and resume their journeys on foot, tramping through the drifting snow as cheerfully as circumstances would allow.

At Bryn Cross, one car was stopped which carried a lady and her four children who were on their way to St Helens. To resume their journey was impossible and the mother resolved to stay all night in the car, she and the children being supplied with hot coffee and eatables from homes near-by.

A couple on their way to Westhoughton had to leave the car at Bryn Cross and trudge the distance on foot. All the routes on the Wigan tramway system stopped and the electric line brush was used with some little success on the Aspull and Gidlow routes. But it was one o'clock on Wednesday afternoon before a car could proceed even the shortest distance to Gidlow Lane. On the Pemberton route, the trams were scotched before nine o'clock on Christmas night, being unable to move, the drifts of snow in many places being over two feet deep, the stoppage of the trams adding to the inconvenience and many people who had been out visiting just could not get to their homes. Parties were glad to avail themselves of shelter at the hands of strangers. On Wednesday night, efforts were made to open the tram lines but as soon as the snow was cleared, it was replaced by fresh falls.

Only two cars ended up running - from the Market Gate to Union Bridge. Many passengers were stranded and one family spent the night in the waiting room of the South Lancashire Tramway Company. Some drivers and conductors had to stay with their vehicles all night because of severe weather. A party of wedding guests had to walk from Worsley to Hindley. In another instance about half a dozen passengers for Hindley were stranded at Bag Lane, Atherton, and spent the night in the cold comfort of the waiting room. In some cases, it took as long as two hours to travel the little distance of one mile.

In the case of colliers who were late, it meant a full days play (in old "Wigan speak" play meant not going to work). A Bamfurlong correspondent writes to say that during the heavy snow storm on Christmas night no less than six of the South West Lancashire cars were blocked between Bamfurlong and Stubshaw Cross. Some of the passengers who lived in Platt Bridge walked home, but others living further away remained in the cars all night.

Many people were enabled to take part in the almost legendary "Christmas bump" this year. In some cases, it was much against their will. Cases of arm breakages and injuries to other parts of the body were reported. It was difficult to walk in some of the steepest parts of the district such as Standishgate Hill and Spring Bank, Pemberton, and where the boys had "slidden" the pathways to the nature of glass, it was positively dangerous. This snow fall would cost the ratepayers hundreds of pounds.

LETTER TO THE EDITOR OF THE WIGAN OBSERVER

New Year's Eve - 1904

Sir,
On reading your paper this week I was surprised to see your remarks on the comparative desertion of the streets on Christmas Eve. I think another story ought to be told. Before coming to reside in Wigan I was told again and again that I was coming to one of the worst towns in Lancashire. This report I refused to accept and for weeks after my arrival felt justified in this unbelief. A few Saturday nights ago I tramped the streets until close to one o'clock in the morning and saw and heard things that filled me with much shame and sorrow, they caused me to reverse my previously formed morality or immorality of the town. My experiences last Saturday night I want to place before your readers in the hope of exciting public opinion against the drunkenness and vice in Wigan. I do not lose sight of the fact that it was Christmas Eve but fail to see this can be any justification for the laxity and looseness of morals which I witnessed. I left our Mission Hall about 9.45 and walked into the town centre by way of Caroline Street. Up to this point I had passed scores and scores of people under the influence of drink the vast majority of whom were very young men and women; many were mere boys and girls.

By the Market Square was a great crowd of men - drunken, quarrelsome, shouting and swearing. On the outskirts of this crowd were many young boys and girls all more or less under the influence of drink. Clumsy and indecent attempts were made to perform the "Cake Walk" and each attempt was followed by a falling into each others arms. Shameless embracing seemed to be the order of the night. Crowds roamed about, shouted and screamed and one very young man we passed was vomiting foul filth on the causeway. He looked to be about 20 and was horribly drunk. From 10.45 until 12.45 I visited the worst neighbourhoods I could find. At least 90 per cent of the people were drunk - and these were people of all ages. In one street, a lot of people were standing about in a state of intoxication. At one house I heard screams and repeated kickings at the door. I walked in and found a poor woman clad in unwomanly rags lying on the floor terribly drunk. She got on her feet and struck a man in the face and gave him what would be a black eye. In the kitchen the floor was littered with broken crockery and food - the mad work of this poor fallen women. Before leaving this street I saw a poor girl too drunk to walk. She was with two young men who were helping her. They disappeared down a yard and were followed at intervals by other men. Later, I saw these men on the streets again. Who were these men? I imagine they had retired to clean and respectable homes while these poor harlot daughters of God were left to drag their corrupt and rotten lives to the prostitute's grave.

I found Hardybutts and Scholes bad but not as bad as I expected. The worst feature of these places was the number of young children aged five, six and seven who were playing in the streets but who ought to have been in bed hours before dreaming of dear old Santa Claus. At after 12.20 I left several lads and lassies sitting or half lying on the forms at the bottom of the Market Square. The cold, damp fog made no difference to them. They remained to catch cold or something worse.

I close this letter by advising members of the Council's Watch Committee to spend New Year's Eve on the Streets and increase the number of police. I might say that policemen seemed scarce on Saturday night. No harm would be done if public houses were closed before 11 o'clock.

I am, Yours very sincerely
W A Harrison
14 Park View
Wigan.

PS: The friends who accompanied me agree with all I have said. We agree more might be written and the saddest features must remain unpublished.

THE DOUGLAS OVERFLOWS AT MARTLAND MILL

The Martland Mill district last week (1909) certainly had the appearance of the Fens about it, the heavy rains causing the River Douglas to overflow. The sketch was done on Monday of the river, which further down runs into the flooded fields on each side. The rainfall in Wigan for Saturday and Sunday was 1.63 inches. In Hindley, the storm caused much damage and the streets in some places were under water and the cellars flooded. The main road between Leigh and Wigan, Twist Lane, was submerged to such a depth that horses refused to go through it and a detour of two miles was necessary. The adjoining houses were flooded and the occupants removed their ground floor furniture upstairs. Firs Lane was impassable, water bubbling up like geysers from manholes. The low-lying land between Plank Lane and Pennington Station resembled a lake. Much damage and inconvenience ensued.

Wicked Wigan 2

WIGAN BOROUGH MAGISTRATES POLICE COURT (1906)

COPYING OTHERS: A small boy named Walter Holland (10) of 4 Bryn Street, Lower Ince, whose case was heard when the court was cleared, was put up on a charge of larceny. The Chief Constable said the lad was respectable and was from good parents. He had a testimonial from the vicar of St Mary's Church, Lower Ince, and he did not think it was the wish of the prosecutrix to go on with the case. He went in the shop on Saturday afternoon and the assistant happened to be out. She heard a rattle in the drawer and caught the lad red-handed. There was one shilling and six pence (7p) missing. The lad said he had seen others do it. The Magistrates advised the parents to punish the boy. He promised to be better in future.

A WOMAN'S ROW: Jane Stothers, of 13 School Lane, was summoned for assaulting Rachel Gaskell of 7 Butler Street, Wigan. Complainant said defendant gave her a thump on the head and knocked her down. Three weeks before there had been other assaults; defendant had no witnesses but said she had never struck her on that date. A fine of five shillings (25p) was imposed.

HUSBAND AND WIFE FIGHTING: James Mayor, a goods guard, of 15 Pennyhurst Street, Wigan, was summoned by his wife Mary, of 2 Wilcock Street, for persistent cruelty. From the complainant's statement, it appeared they had been married for 21 years and had seven children. Defendant had often beaten her and owing to his conduct, she left him. A son said that his father often ill-used his mother. Defendant said some papers had gone out of the house and he wanted them back. He was going to be master in his own house. The case was adjourned for three weeks, and Mr Anders, the missionary, was asked to talk to the parties.

SUNDAY GAMBLING: Peter Lee, 22, Sarginson Street and Ralph Parkinson, 6 Albert Street, were summoned for gaming with cards; and Elias Houghton, 18 Kildare Street and John Gaskell, 41 Ormskirk Road were summoned for aiding and abetting. They pleaded guilty. Police Constable Roberts (65) saw Lee and Parkinson playing cards on Sunday and at the end of the game the two other defendants received a share of the money. They were each fined one shilling (5p) and costs.

ALARMING GAS EXPLOSION IN WIGAN

A serious gas explosion occurred at a house in Spring Grove, off Darlington Street, Wigan, on Monday evening (July 1902). The occupier Elias Birchall and Hugh McGirl, who lodges with him, returned home about 11.30pm and there was a strong smell of gas. McGirl went into the parlour to turn off the gas at the meter. Birchall struck a match and an explosion at once took place.

The windows were blown out, the parlour door broken and the ceiling was damaged and the two men were badly burned about the face and arms. The whole force was not expended here for it travelled through the kitchen and bulged out the walls of the wash-house and in the bedroom upstairs.

The occupants of adjoining houses received a rude shock and were exceedingly alarmed. One case is reported of a person in a house close by being thrown from the bed to the floor.

Police Constable Blackledge went to the scene after hearing the sound of breaking glass. He saw flames coming from the window of No 7. He saw the men who were taken into the house and their burns attended to. Birchall was the worst burned of the two and is going on as well as can be expected.

A POISONING CASE AT HINDLEY

A widow named Mary Pears, 60 years old, of Liverpool Road, Hindley, died on Monday in consequence of taking oxalic acid. It appears that shortly after 6 o'clock in the evening, the daughter of the deceased found her lying on the sofa. She was vomiting and she said she had taken the acid. Information was given to the police and the usual remedies resorted to but it was found that the woman was unable to swallow. It appears that she had been in delicate health for some months.

Mr S Brighouse, the Coroner, held an inquest at the Strangeways Hotel at Hindley on Wednesday when Harriet Fisher, the daughter, said the previous Monday night she had words about sixpence which her husband said she had taken. She denied this but her husband went to the public house and found that she had bought six pennyworth of whiskey.

Her husband came back and to settle the matter, witness gave him a shilling. He said later that he was on the jury of an inquest that morning and she said "It'll be on me." She said it so many times before but she did not think she would take her life.

Instead of going to the inquest to serve on the jury, the man went drinking at a public house.

Coroner: Being a juryman, this must have had a demoralising affect on him.

Witness said she told her mother to go out for fear of more rows. When she went to the public house, someone fetched her and said her mother was ill.

Answering Inspector Pickering, witness said her mother tried to poison herself six years ago. Her mother used the acid to take iron mould out of linen.

The jury returned a verdict of suicide.

STARTLING DISCOVERY AT INCE

A startling discovery was made at Ince on Saturday (1906). A youth was playing on the canal bank and throwing a hook into the water he was soon aware that it had become attached to something. Pulling the hook out, he was surprised to find fastened to it a greater part of a woman's leg on which were a stocking and a boot. As a result of grappling, another boot was drawn from the water, this being similar to the one on the leg. It was reported that some men had found the other leg. The canal has been further grappled but no information of any fresh discovery has transpired. It is supposed that the remains found are part of the body of a married woman who had been missing from Lower Ince for some time.

FINED FOR SHEBEENING

At Standish Court on Thursday, John Spencer, of Preston Road, was summoned for having sold intoxicating liquor without a licence.

John Taylor, beer and mineral water bottler, of Heath Road, Ashton, was brought up for aiding and abetting. He was also charged with selling intoxicating liquors without a licence, and Martin Flynn was summoned for illegally dealing.

Mr Lees stated that in consequence of the suspicions of the police, the wife of Police Constable Williams was sent to Spencer's house at 11-14 at night and was supplied with a pint bottle of stout. Other similar cases were stated.

The case against Taylor was dismissed. The other defendants were fined £5.

EDWARDIAN CRUELTY

SAD CHRISTMAS FATALITY AT GOOSE GREEN.

BURNED WHILST EXAMINING PLAYTHINGS.

A very sad accident happened on Christmas morning at Goose Green which resulted in the death of a child named Mary Jane Grocott, aged seven. Deceased was the daughter of William Henry Grocott, of 49, Bentinck-street, and at half-past five on Christmas morning the child, with her sister Annie, aged 8, got out of bed for the purpose of examining their stockings, which were hanging at the foot of the bed. They contained, amongst other things, two small wax candles. The children asked their parents to allow them to go downstairs where there was a fire. They were told not to go, and the father and mother then went to sleep. They were awakened at ten minutes past seven by screams which came from the kitchen. On going downstairs the deceased was found with her clothes on fire. The father, with the assistance of a neighbour, extinguished the flames and applied oil and limewater. Dr. Wolstenholme was sent for, and he attended the little girl until she died at five minutes to one on Tuesday morning. It appears that the children went downstairs and deceased lighted a piece of paper. She then attempted to light one of the candles, and threw down the paper, when her clothes became ignited.

THE INQUEST.

Mr. H. Milligan, borough coroner, held the inquest at the New Inn, Goose Green, on Wednesday.

Wm. Henry Grocott, father of the deceased, said after the deceased and her sister had asked him if they could go downstairs he went to sleep again, and the next thing he heard was a scream in the kitchen. The girl Annie told him the deceased lighted a piece of paper and threw it on the floor, and it must have set her clothes on fire.

Elizabeth Grocott corroborated this statement. She could not get anything out of the deceased. Witness had never seen her children play with lighted paper.

Noah Kinsey, the next door neighbour, said he heard screams about ten minutes past seven on Christmas morning. When he went into Grocott's he found the deceased in flames. Mr. Grocott was then downstairs, and witness assisted him to put them out with a blanket.

Annie Grocott, a girl of eight, who gave her evidence in a very intelligent manner, said when they got downstairs her sister lighted a piece of paper at

THE DANGERS OF THE DOLLY TUB.

ANOTHER CHILD DROWNED.

Another has been added to the already long list of juvenile victims to the wash tub. Another child has been drowned in the dolly-tub in this district—this time at Hindley. Its name was Charles Simm, and it was the year and ten months' old son of Samuel Simm, 5, Martin-street, Hindley. An inquest was held by Mr. Coroner Brighouse, at the Royal Hotel, Hindley, on Tuesday afternoon. The mother, Ellen Simm, described how the infant met with its death. It was playing in the yard, she said, trying to sail a salmon tin in some water that was in a tub. When it had been out of the house about a quarter of an hour she looked and discovered it head downwards in the tub. The infant had fallen into the water while endeavouring to reach the can, which was also in the water. Artificial respiration was tried, but without avail. The tub was nineteen inches long and fourteen inches wide, and at the time it contained only six inches of water. A verdict of "Accidental death" was returned.

THE STANDISH BUTCHER AND HIS LOST BEEF.

At the Chorley Sessions, on Tuesday week, a man named William Trafford was charged with stealing two pieces of meat, value 1s. 8d., belonging to John Bentham, butcher, Preston-road, Standish. Mr. Callis defended prisoner.—Prosecutor said on Friday, the 4th inst., he had a conveyance containing meat for sale at Almond Brook, Shevington. He called at the Foresters' Arms, leaving his horse and cart in the lane. He had a glass of beer to drink. When he went into the house there were a lot of pieces of meat in the cart, but he could not swear he had a shoulder of lamb in his cart when he went into the public-house. When he came out of the house he missed a piece of beef about 2½lbs. weight, and from what was said he went to the prisoner, who was in the public-house, and said to him "If thou doesn'd find that beef I shall have thee locked up." Prisoner replied that he had not taken any. Witness then gave information to the police. The

BURNING AT ASHTON

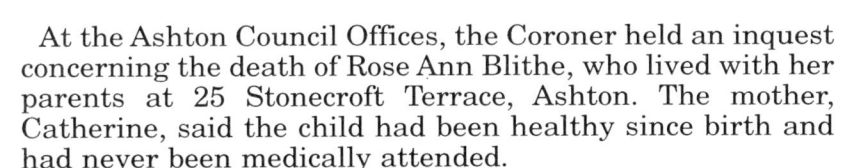

At the Ashton Council Offices, the Coroner held an inquest concerning the death of Rose Ann Blithe, who lived with her parents at 25 Stonecroft Terrace, Ashton. The mother, Catherine, said the child had been healthy since birth and had never been medically attended.

About a couple of months ago, she and her husband and the child were in the kitchen. The fender was down and the child fell with her right arm on the top bar of the grate. There was a small burn and she got some soap and put it on the part. Afterwards, she put some liniment on and the wound seemed to heal. The child, however, kept scratching her arm and caused several small sores to appear which did not heal. But on Friday she said she felt poorly and witness put her downstairs in the cradle and gave her some magnesia in the evening. But she did not improve and Dr Garrett was called in and gave her some medicine.

She gradually grew worse and died on Sunday morning.

In answer to the Coroner, the mother said she put a piece of the best white soap on the spot. The Coroner remarked that he asked the question because there were some soaps which contained poisoning matter. The mother, continuing, said the child had a swelling under the right arm which she had noticed, thinking it was the natural fat of the child. When the doctor came, he discovered the swelling and said the child was going to have an abscess.

Coroner: Why did you let her keep picking the sore?

Witness: I wrapped it up many a time but she kept picking the rag off.

Coroner: You ought to have tied the other hand up so she could not have done it.

A verdict of accidental death was returned.

KILLED BY MOTOR CAR

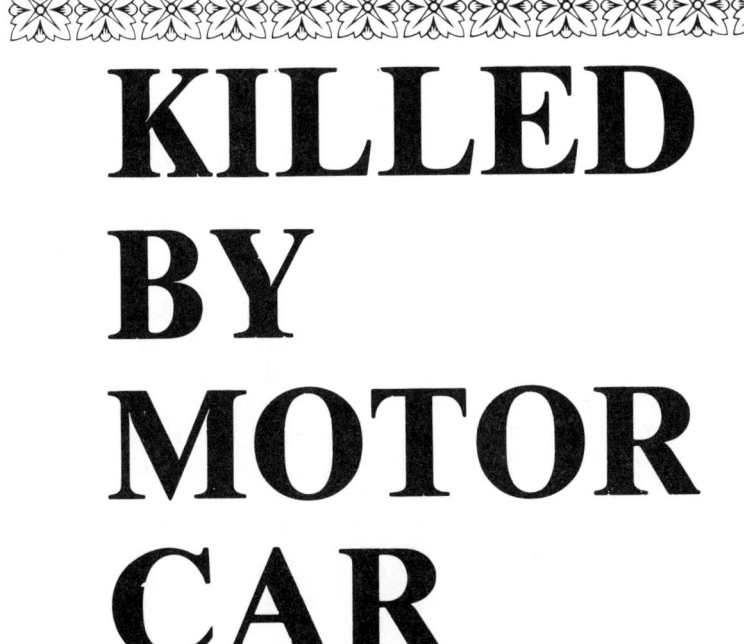

Mr R W Ascroft, the Deputy Coroner, conducted an inquest at the Police Station on Monday on to the body of John Waterhouse, 73, retired factory operative, of Byron Street, Lower Ince, who while crossing Standishgate on Friday was knocked over by a motor car.

Miss Margaret Tomlinson, of Bamber Bridge, said that at about 3.30pm she left the doctor's surgery and was crossing over the road when she noticed a motor car coming in the other direction and at the same time saw the deceased in the middle of the road. The old man, even when about three yards from the car, did not see it and appeared quite dazed.

It was only when the car was on top of him that he seemed to realise his position and then instead of turning in the right direction, turned into the car. She next saw the car swerve on to the footpath and the old man lay in the road.

Coroner: At what speed was the car travelling?

Witness: I could not say but it was very slowly.

Juryman: Did the car sound any alarm?

Witness: I did not hear any.

Mary Hornby said the car was travelling at not more than walking pace.

The Coroner heard that the deceased seemed to be dazed and Edwin Blackburn, the chauffeur, said he was driving at about seven or eight miles an hour. On seeing the deceased standing in the middle of the road, he sounded his horn several times and slowed down to about walking pace. The deceased stopped in the road and looked towards the car. By this time, they had come within four yards of him and in order to avoid catching him, he turned the car on to the footpath. The back part of the car, however, caught the deceased and knocked him down.

The jury returned a verdict of accidental death.

SAD BURNING ON CHRISTMAS EVE

A little girl named Jeraldine Morris, aged four years, of Preston Road, Standish, daughter of Martha Morris, has come by her death through being burned, under circumstances necessitating an inquest.

The inquest was held by Mr Parker at the Wheatsheaf Hotel Standish.

From the evidence, it appeared that at about half past two in the afternoon of Christmas Eve (1903), the mother left the little girl in the parlour with another girl named Ethel Tranter, five years of age. There was a fire in the grate and the mother leaving them, cautioned them not to go near it.

When Mrs Morris left, she went into the scullery to attend to her work and shortly afterwards she was startled on hearing Ethel shout "Jeraldine's on fire."

The mother ran into the parlour and found her little daughter in flames and attempted to put out these with her hands. When failing to, she rushed for water and threw it over the child, thus extinguishing the flames.

The child was badly burned and a doctor sent for. In about twenty minutes, Dr Ormsby, assistant to Dr Wilson, was in attendance and the suffering child was tended by him until she died shortly before ten o'clock three days later.

STANDISH VIDEO

Video Presentations by **Geoffrey Shryhane** *Filmed by* **Steve Balfour**

The Old Market Hall & Demolition Of Wigan Cooling Towers £14

The Lowry Centenary At Salford Art Gallery...................................£10

The Life And Work Of The Artist Tom Dodson..............................£10

AVAILABLE BY POST
(Add 60p)

From: **Standish Video, 26 Market Street, Standish, Wigan. Tel: 0257 426937**

The jury returned a verdict to the effect that the child died from her injuries caused by burning and that death was accidental.

The Coroner, at the close of the inquiry, mentioned that was the third inquest he had attended that day through the same cause and recommended that where there were young children, parents should prevent similar happenings by providing fire guards so that the infants could not get "afire."

CHRISTMAS FATALITY AT GOOSE GREEN

A very sad accident happened on Christmas morning (1905) at Goose Green which resulted in the death of a child named Mary Ann Grocott, aged seven, of Bentinck Street. At half past seven on Christmas morning the child, with her sister, Annie, aged eight, got out of bed for the purpose of examining their stockings, which were hanging at the foot of the bed. They contained, amongst other things, two small wax candles. The children asked their parents to allow them to go downstairs where there was a fire. They were told not to go and the father and mother went back to sleep.

THE WIGAN GALLERIES

Shopping Centre

- ONE STOP SHOPPING IN THE HEART OF TOWN
- TOP NAME STORES
- SMALL SPECIALITY SHOPS
- INDOOR & OUTDOOR MARKET
- TOP CHOICE & VALUE
- PARKING FOR 660 CARS

You can't afford to miss us.

The gateway to a new shopping experience

CIN Properties Limited

They were awakened at ten minutes past seven by screams which came from the kitchen. On going downstairs, the deceased was found with her clothes on fire. The father, with the assistance of a neighbour, extinguished the flames and applied oil and lime water. Dr Wolstenholme was sent for and he attended the little girl until she died at five minutes to one on Tuesday morning. It appears that the children went downstairs and the deceased lighted a piece of paper. She then attempted to light one of the candles, and threw down the paper when her clothes became ignited.

The Inquest

Mr Milligan, the Borough Coroner held the inquest at the New Inn, Goose Green, on Wednesday. Wm Henry Grocott said after the deceased and her sister had asked him if they could go downstairs, he went to sleep again and the next thing he heard was a scream. The girl Annie told him the deceased's clothes caught fire after she threw the lighted piece of paper on the floor.

Annie, who gave her evidence in a very intelligent manner, said when they got downstairs, her sister lighted a piece of paper at the fire and lit one of the candles with it. She then threw the paper on the floor and witness thought it had gone out but when she turned round, she saw her sister's clothing on fire. They had never played with lighted paper before and witness said she would never do so again.

A verdict of Accidental Death was returned.

Experience Tropical Butterfly World
at
CANNELLS Garden Centre

Whatever the weather, step into the luxuriant atmosphere of the tropics!
See a dazzling delight of flying jewels, exotic plants, terrapins, fish and birds in a creatively arranged setting.

Choose from our extensive range of quality house plants.	We stock a wide range of shrubs and hardy outdoor plants too!

Relax and finalise your shopping list in our Coffee Shop, where refreshing beverages and tasty snacks are available.

We are situated adjacent to Junction 27 of the M6 in Back Lane, Appley Bridge, just off the A5209 Parbold/Standish Road. Telephone: 0257 423355

WIGAN COTTON SPINNERS FINED

A child of 12, described as a scavenger, seriously injured his finger while illegally cleaning a machine at a Wigan cotton mill.

At the Wigan Borough Court, Thomas Taylor and Brothers Ltd of Victoria Mills, Wallgate, were brought before the justices for an offence under the Factory and Workshops Act for allowing a child to clean machinery.

Mr C Appleton pleaded guilty on behalf of the company.

Mr R Tinker, His Majesty's Inspector of Factories, who prosecuted, stated the section of the act under which the proceedings were taken. He said that a child must not be allowed to clean machinery whether it was in motion or at rest.

On November 26 (1903), the boy, Henry Morley, aged 12, was allowed to clean machinery in motion and his finger was injured.

The boy gave evidence and said he was at his usual work and was told to clean the carriage wheel by a miner, Fred Oxley. While doing so, his finger was badly injured.

Mr Bolton, for the firm, said the boy was a scavenger who had to sweep up. It was a fact that he did touch the machine and had his finger slightly injured but the management knew nothing of it.

The boy went on working and it was a total surprise when they were informed of the finger injury. They were very sorry about that.

Mr Appleton said strict attention would be paid so that children would not get too near machinery in the future.

The magistrates imposed a fine of ten shillings (50p) and costs.

Wicked Wigan 2

●MESNES STREET● TELEPHONE 42810 - 46270 STD 0942●

Wigan's Original Bookshop

smiths of wigan

• *the better choice* •

●MESNES STREET● TELEPHONE 42810 - 46270 STD 0942●

WIGAN WOMAN'S SUICIDE ATTEMPT

At the Borough Police Court before Messrs J M Ainscough and J Peterkin, a woman named Martha Pennington, of 19 Yates Street was charged with attempting to commit suicide using salts of lemon.

Inspector Wright said the prisoner had been living since two years prior to her husband's death with a man who, it appeared, had been abusing her. He struck her on Tuesday, giving her a black eye, and it was in a fit of passion, probably brought on by such treatment, that she went and purchased some salts of lemon, mixed it and drank it. She was seen by a neighbour shortly after having taken it and given an emetic (a medicine to make her vomit) and was then brought to the police station where she was seen by Dr Roocroft.

Elizabeth Wood, a neighbour, said that at about four o'clock on Tuesday afternoon she went to the prisoner's house and there saw her sitting in a chair. She asked what was the matter and the prisoner replied "Oh my. I have done it. I have supped some poison. It is through him."

The Bench heard that the prisoner had a sister living in Prescot who it was thought would look after her.

WALMSLEYS
INSURANCE

Insurance Brokers & Independent Financial Advisers

The Walmsley Promise:

✧ Competitive Premiums.

✧ Professional expertise from qualified staff.

✧ First class claims settlement - plus a full uninsured loss recovery service including car hire for motor claims.

✧ Excellent local personal service at all times.

Insurance Brokers and Independent Financial Advisers

WALMSLEY HOUSE, 35 DICCONSON STREET,
WIGAN, WN1 2AS.
Telephone 43455 (20 lines)

Life and Pensions Office:
71 DICCONSON STREET, WIGAN, WN1 2AS.
Telephone: 826996

The Magistrates remanded her until the following day.

The prisoner was brought before the Mayor and other Magistrates on Thursday.

The Chief Constable said her sister declined to have anything to do with her and none of her friends who had many times tried to redeem her would help.

The Bench discharged her on condition that she went to the workhouse.

GOLBORNE BIGAMIST

At Liverpool Assizes on Tuesday, Samuel Grundy, aged 54, a collier, was charged with having committed bigamy at Golborne on January 25th, 1897.

It was stated that the prisoner was married to Elizabeth Thomas at Bolton in 1875 and in 1897 he went through a form of marriage with Ada Else at Golborne, his wife being then, and still, alive. Ada Else said she had eight children by the prisoner, seven of them being alive. Twelve months ago, he deserted her and since then she had been in the workhouse.

Mr Griffiths, appearing for the prisoner, said he had elicited the fact that the prisoner's wife had also married for a second time, some time after the prisoner had gone through the ceremony with Else. Counsel submitted that the prisoner had good reason to believe that his wife was dead when he contracted the second marriage.

The police records showed that the prisoner had several times been guilty of cruelty and neglect to both of the women with whom he had lived. He was sentenced to three years' penal servitude.

Observer

Now you've enjoyed the book you can keep in touch with Geoffrey every week in the Wigan Observer

Geoffrey Shryhane and the Wigan Observer
A Winning Combination

Martland Mill ● Martland Mill Lane
Wigan ● WN5 0LX ● Tel: 228000

DOMESTIC PROBLEMS AT WIGAN

There was subdued laughter at Wigan Police Court when a young woman said she did not mind her husband thumping her but drew the line at kicking.

At the Court, a young man named Joseph Garry, of 24 Stuart Street, Wigan, was summoned for persistent cruelty to his wife, Catherine Garry, who lived at 25 Ashton Street. He pleaded not guilty.

Mrs Garry's statement was that they had been married just over twelve months and she had two children. He had been cruel to her ever since they were married. She could stand being thumped but not kicked. He had also ran her out of the house with a knife. She admitted that defendant

The Hallgate Press

High Quality Lithographic Printers

Eckersley's No.3 Mill,
Swan Meadow Road, Wigan WN3 5AZ.
0942 496442

did not like her mother, but his mother had beaten her and he had helped.

Dismissing the case, Alderman Richards advised them to get away from their mothers-in-law.

HUSBAND'S TROUSERS PAWNED

At Wigan Magistrates' Court, Thomas Lowe, of 85 Caroline Street, Wigan, denied that he had deserted his wife Agnes, of 57 York Street.

Complainant said they had been married for 27 years and there were five children under 16 years of age. He left her twelve months last march and would only give her seven shillings a week (35p) which was not enough.

Inspector Malone, of the NSPCC, said the woman was indolent and the husband had made several complaints about her drunkenness. He had to tear his clothes so that she could not pawn them. She had pawned them often before. He found doubtful associates in the house the worse for drink.

The Chairman said the man had better take the children away from her. The Magistrates would make a separation order, the defendant to give his wife four shillings (20p).

TURN YOUR SCRAP INTO CASH

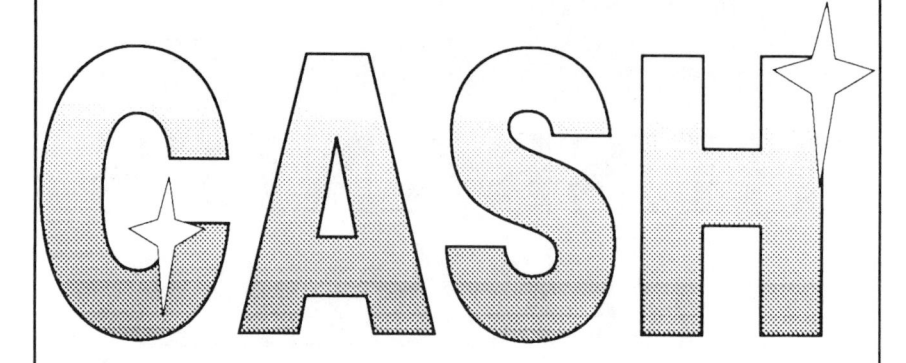

BITHELL'S

SCRAP PROCESSORS (WIGAN)
ESTABLISHED OVER 20 YEARS
FOR TOP PRICES & PROMPT PAYMENTS

* FACTORIES AND ENGINEERING CLEARANCE
* FERROUS AND NON-FERROUS METALS
* WASTE DISPOSAL SKIP HIRE
* SKIPS PROVIDED * COLLECTION SERVICE
* WEIGHBRIDGE CHECKED BY LOCAL AUTHORITY
* 24 HOUR ANSWERING SERVICE

WIGAN (0942) 48965
FAX: (0942) 820238

THE OLD BREWERY, WESTWOOD
ROAD, WIGAN. WN3 5DE

AND FINALLY...

Mrs Wilkinson (From a photo).

This is the best test of truth. Here is a Wigan story which has stood the test of time. It is a story with a point which will come straight home to many of us. It was three years ago that Mrs Wilkinson began using Doan's Backache Kidney Pills and the following statement which she then made gives the details of her then serious illness.

PEERLESS

Central Lancashire Printers Ltd

Specialist newspaper contract printers

MARTLAND MILL, WIGAN

"A couple of years ago I had the misfortune to catch cold after childbirth and a violent pain attacked me in the left side. I was treated by two doctors but in the end they said there was no hope of saving my life. I then went into Wigan Infirmary where I was subjected to hot baths and injections. This treatment however only weakened me and all the time my body was growing larger. At last the doctor decided to "tap" me and 19 ozs of water were taken away. But my body soon began to fill again. I was discharged from the Infirmary as incurable and I returned home feeling that I could not live long. Another doctor was called in and he said that the only thing he could do was to "tap" me which he did, removing 10 quarts of water. He had no hope, though, and I could feel myself filling again.

I felt as though I should suffocate. The doctor again "tapped" me taking away, 12 quarts of water this time.

But it was the same thing over again. I got as bad as ever I had been. Just then I heard of a case similar to mine having been cured by Doan's Backache Kidney Pills. And I determined to try the pills myself. I used them at the rate of one box a week and soon I could tell the pills were doing me good and the water in my body lessened.

In four weeks' time I was able to leave my bed and each week, each day, I could feel myself improving. The terrible pressure on my heart was relieved. A few months later, I was so well that my friends could scarcely believe I was the same woman. I think my cure is splendid evidence that Doan's pills are a true kidney medicine.

Mrs R Wilkinson, 27 Spring Gardens, Frog Lane, Wigan, says: "The cure of my dropsy by Doan's Backache Kidney Pills has indeed proved a lasting one as I am still well. I cannot say too much in praise of Doan's Pills for I am sure they have saved my life. I have recommended the medicine to many people and I hope the publication of my case will be the means of bringing relief to other sufferers."

Doan's Backache Kidney Pills are 2s 9dp (17p) a box from all chemists and stores, or post free direct from Foster - McClellan Co., 8 Wells Street, Oxford Street, London. Be sure you get exactly the same kind of pills that Mrs Wilkinson had.

WIGAN LITTLE THEATRE

Crompton Street, Wigan, WN1 3SL. Tel: 42561
Member of the Little Theatre Guild of Great Britain

ADVANCE BOOKINGS

At box office (Tel: 0942 42561)
Monday - Friday, 7.00 - 9.00pm
Saturday, 10.00 - 12 noon

See LOCAL PRESS for details of shows

STEP BACK IN TIME AND LIVE THE LIFE OF 1900!

We can take you back in time to the year 1900, where you can experience life in a Victorian classroom, the pub, the cottage, the coalmine, and even journey to Blackpool – all without leaving Wigan.

WIGAN PIER, WIGAN
Opening times may vary - Please ring for details
Telephone: 0942 323666
ALWAYS THE FAMILY FAVOURITE